Essential Knowledge for a First Year Audit Staff/Intern in a Big 4 Accounting

A TRUE INSIDER'S PERSPECTIVE ON BIG 4 ACCOUNTING

ISBN-13: 978-1481097048
ISBN-10: 1481097040

CONTENTS

About The Author

Kevin H graduated Cum Laude from University of California, Irvine with a Bachelors of Arts in Economics and Minor in Accounting. He is a Certified Public Accountant and has worked in a Big 4 public accounting firm (i.e. Ernst & Young, KPMG, Deloitte, or PwC) for about three years primarily servicing clients in the credit services and life sciences/pharmaceuticals industries. However, he has experience in the automotive, electronics, and private equity industries as well. Prior to working in the Big 4, Kevin held a finance position at The Boeing Company.

Since 2005, he has been successfully trading stocks on the side - achieving high single digit to double digit returns each year. He combines fundamental analysis with technical analysis in determining which stocks to trade and when to trade them. His time frame ranges from days to three months.

In addition, he also spent some time working at an investment banking firm, which focused on mergers and acquisitions. In addition, he is the owner of StockKevin.com, a personal growth, stock trading, and financial savvy site. When he is not working, Kevin enjoys golfing, rock climbing, meditation, and yoga.

When you think of an accountant, typically, you think of someone who prepares tax returns or is a pure number cruncher. While this might have been true in the past, nowadays we have Microsoft Excel to help us crunch numbers. But, accounting is much more than that. Stricter government regulations such as the implementation of the Sarbanes-Oxley Act have paved the way for greater demands in different careers within the accounting field. Below are a few sub-categories within the accounting field to consider.

Audit: Auditors perform procedures to ensure company's financial statements are free from material misstatements. In addition, they ensure that the financial statements accurately reflect the financial performance of the company they are auditing. Banks and lenders request companies be audited because they want to be reassured that companies they lend to will be able to pay their debts. Public companies file reports such as the 10K and 10Q with the SEC. Investors factor into their decision making process the information in these reports. Naturally, companies will have an incentive to overstate their assets and understate their liabilities. Therefore it is important to have a third party, such as an auditor to ensure that the banks and investors are protected.

Tax: Tax professionals prepare tax returns both on an individual and corporate basis. This includes international, federal, state, and local tax returns. In these economic times, companies are looking to reduce their tax liabilities and make better investment decisions. Tax regulations are constantly changing. This is largely due to the direction the government decides to take the economy. For example, the housing market has been on a decline in recent years. In order to mitigate this situation, the government has decided to provide tax credits to first time homeowners to boost the housing market. Tax professionals are aware of such recent developments and would be able to effectively advise individuals.

Information Technology (IT): As the world moves towards more and more sophisticated software systems, the need for individuals with IT knowledge continues to grow alongside it. Accounting systems' design complexities have increased in recent years and require extensive knowledge to troubleshoot. Professionals continue to design and implement advanced software systems. Individuals with skills to manipulate, design, and implement such systems are extremely valuable to companies.

Internal Audit: Although similar in duties to an external auditor, internal auditors focus on ensuring their company's internal controls are functioning properly. In some cases, they will perform similar procedures to that of an external auditor. An internal auditor is directly associated with their company and thus not considered a third party. Therefore, companies will have to employ another company to ensure their financial statements are free from material misstatements. Where internal auditor's value lies is in the fact that they will be able to large issues before they reach the external auditors. Therefore, cut down the work needed from external auditors, effectively reducing audit fees.

Forensics: Accounting professionals perform procedures to detect white collar crime such as fraud, tax evasion, and embezzlement.

International Focus: With exception to countries like the United States, much of the world is under IFRS (International Financial Reporting Standards). Globalization has moved the United States to consider IFRS Standards. There have been advanced talks regarding the inclusion of IFRS standards in the CPA exam. Professionals with IFRS experience will become valuable to companies within the United States as well as across the globe in the coming years.

Consulting: This involves financial planning, organizational restructuring, and management tactics. Individuals will leverage prior years' data and knowledge of the current business environment to plan for the future.

General Accounting: Accountants are responsible for general ledgers, trial balances, financial statements and other general accounting issues. Often these same individuals will be responsible for closing the books at year end. Furthermore, it is not uncommon to see reconciliations from the detail listings to the trial balances be a part of their duties.

Busy season as you may or may not be are aware of is a period in time during the year when auditors are most busy. How many hours do you work during this time? To put things in perspective, I've put in 350 hours of work in March. If you are working Monday through Friday, 350 hours in a month is about 15 hours a day. Is this typical? Honestly, the number of hours you work depends on what clients you are put on, but the best it can get during busy season is 55 hour weeks. Basically, if you are working in public accounting, get ready for long hours.

When is busy season? Busy season is from January through April.

Busy season is the reason why we have our jobs. Companies public companies issue 10Qs every quarter, but the firms don't necessarily do an audit. Instead we do a review of the quarter. The difference between a review and audit is that there are more inquiries, balance sheet & income statement analytics, and less substantive work in general. We want to see if there is anything that is unexpected and understand why there are changes from prior quarter over current quarter, prior year-end quarter over current year quarter, and year to date over year to date.

Also if there is something that we can do now versus at year-end we would review that. For example, if there is an acquisition, we will likely perform procedures over that acquisition now rather than at year-end. This is to move work forward and lessen the load at year-end. Of course not everything can be moved up to an interim date. Cash confirmations need to be confirmed as of the year-end date.

Partners opine on the client's yearly financial statements. Therefore it makes sense that we are most busy after the client closes their final month. Clients have tight deadlines to release their 10K report to the public. The reason it is called busy season is because we work at least eleven hour days for the first three or four months of the year to meet these deadlines.

Auditing has transformed over the years to become much more detailed. In the past if we needed to validate the existence and accuracy of cash and cash equivalents balance, there was not a methodology in place to do so. In other words, it was highly judgmental and confirmations were not sent to all the banks. Nowadays, most firms will send confirmations to all banks. It isn't efficient to test the entire revenue balance especially if it is a multi-billion dollar company with transactions as small as $10. Therefore, firms have developed templates to help determine sample sizes for testing revenue, fixed assets, etc. Otherwise, we would be auditing until the end of the world.

Firms have developed sampling methodologies to either project to the total population or obtain comfort over the majority of the balance. Even with a materiality threshold, there is a lot of work to do. We drill down to the transaction level and obtain support such as third party purchase orders, shipping confirmations, invoices, etc.

The PCAOB has tightened up on the firms to document the procedures we performed. This includes specifically writing down which invoice we looked at and even going down to the date of the invoice. The general rule of thumb is that our documentation needs to be up to reperformance standards. This means another auditor can read what procedures we performed and reperform the procedures. You can guess that many times the actual documentation takes a longer than performing the procedures.

You can guess that many times the actual documentation takes a longer than performing the procedures.

Because we usually work over eleven hours during busy season, the team will order dinner and eat it at the client site. Usually the least senior person will have to pick up the food. Alternatively we have third party restaurant delivery service that will take our order and deliver to the client site. This is different from your normal staying up late studying night. Sitting in front of a computer for ungodly hours can get very tiresome. Imagine sitting in a conference room with a table that barely fits five people but you have six. It's the eleventh hour and the client has been gone for about five hours now. You've been working on a test and at the same time you are trying to juggle giving guidance to an intern or lesser experienced associate.

The first couple days you are fine, but after a couple weeks of this you start to feel the effects. Suddenly your one cup of coffee per day is not enough and three cups are needed to stay awake. It's an intense experience for someone who has not been through it before. You are with the same people for eleven plus hours. We are not talking about each of you having your own personal space. We are all sharing each other's space. You can see that if you don't get along with someone, it could make your experience a long one.

Time passes very quickly as it is, but when you are as busy as you are during busy season; it seems to go by twice as fast. For example, you come into work, get set up, answer emails, coordinate meetings, perform some detailed tests, then all of a sudden its lunch. After lunch you detail test, coach associates, answer emails, perform more detailed tests. Then suddenly it's five, but because it busy season you probably won't even notice. Five o' clock becomes six then seven and then nine and then twelve. The day is over, but you could still be in front of your computer. Finally when you retire for the night, just know you will have to do it again the next day.

If you think that you can catch up on the weekends, think again. This is not always the case, but more likely than not you will probably be working on the weekends. These are typically not full days, but can be depending on your jobs. You can see why it is important to push work forward and do as much as you can when it is not busy. I can't say that busy season is something you can prepare for mentally. Unless you've gone through the experience, something similar, or much worse; you can only anticipate how you will react. Truthfully, it is not about the hours. It is more about the amount of work, pressure, and the fact that you are with the same people for countless hours. It makes a big difference if you are in a room with someone you are coworker friendly with versus someone that you don't get along with.

The following is a description of a busy season day as experienced by an Assurance Associate at one of the Big Four firms:

7:00am - I roll out of my bed and hit the alarm simultaneously. I head to the kitchen and mix some instant oatmeal mix with hot water and grab a piece of bread. As I wait for my oatmeal to cool, I dress for work and make sure I have my laptop, wallet, keys, phone, and sack lunch. Seven minutes in, my oatmeal has not cooled yet, but in the interest of time, I decide to finish it anyways. Afterwards, I brush my teeth, do my hair, and shave.

7:30am - I realize that I am already late, so I rush out of the house only to unsurprisingly hit freeway traffic.

8:30am - After navigating through the heavy traffic, I arrive at the client site. We were given badges for entry into the gated building on Monday. I open the gate with the badge and then walk through another door that requires a badge for entry.

8:45am- I walk into the audit conference room the client has situated us in for the three weeks. I find that two other associates have already arrived. I quickly find my seat and set up my laptop and internet connection. I take out all my necessary writing utensils and notepad.

9:00am - After scanning my emails for anything needing an immediate response, I note nothing pressing. What a letdown. I kid. Typically, I check all my e-mails as I receive them on my cellphone, but I left my phone uncharged the day before. Next, I go down my amassed question list for the client and make sure I understand what I am asking the client and prepare myself mentally for the push back they might give for my requests for supporting documents.

9:25am - I walk upstairs, track down one of my client contacts, and then casually ask her how she is doing this fine sunny morning. After about three minutes of small talk, I crafty segue into my long list of questions. First up on the list is having her explain the variance in unbilled AR balance when comparing prior year figures to current year figures. As I ask these questions I am taking brief notes and asking follow up questions as to receive clarification. I thank her for her time and rush to meet with another client contact.

10:30am - I track down another one of my client contacts on the same floor. This time it's with regards to an AR confirmation discrepancy. The client's customer returned a confirmation for $2M less than the invoice amount. I gain an understanding of the situation and why there is a $2M dispute. The client explains that the customer believes there was a system error that recorded on the invoice more of the product than was requested and delivered. However, the client believes otherwise. I scribble notes on my notepad, so I can interpret the information at a later time.

10:50am - I follow up with a third client contact regarding payroll controls testing. The first time around I did not receive proper support for an employee termination. The control reads that terminations require two levels of manager approval, while I only received support showing one level of manager approval. The client says that they mistakenly left out the information in the support she has sent previously. Just wonderful, I think to myself. She says she will have to follow up with her contact in New Zealand.

11:00am - I update my list of follow ups with the three client contacts I had just conversed with. Some of my other client contacts are pushing back and I will have to return in the afternoon when they believe they will have more time. I set up an appointment with one of the client contacts to meet later today at 4:30pm.

11:30am - A whole morning is almost gone just from chasing the client around for support and explanations. I get back to the audit conference room and my senior asks me for a status update. I give him a status update including what items are open and the reason for them being open. I also explain to him about the progress I've made in the morning. He acknowledges and thanks me for the update.

11:45am - I document what I had just learned from the client in my accounts receivable unbilled step. I do a quick self-check to ensure that I've addressed the tailored procedures, all the document links are linking to the intended areas, including firm templates and filled them out completely, and documented my work to the extent in which it can be readily re-performed by another auditor. I mark the step complete, knowing that I will be receiving coaching notes when I senior reviews the step.

12:00pm - I grab my sack lunch I brought from home from the client's fridge. I eat my lunch in an unused conference room and savor my quick twenty minute break away from the computer. Some of the team members decide to eat at their desks, while others are still on the phone with their client contacts.

12:20pm - It's back to work before 12:30pm and I continue to work on my assigned steps. One of the steps I am assigned is the search for unrecorded liabilities step. I've been in contact with the client, but have not been able to obtain the correct disbursement listing. The client is unsure as to how to generate a simple disbursement listing. I ask the client to follow up with her contact and figure out the situation before getting back to me. In the meantime, I have the payment and invoice support to perform procedures to the extent possible.

2:30pm - I continue to document procedures I performed in my assigned steps and build on my list of follow up questions for the client. I set up an analytics template, which includes developing an expectation and investigating any differences that may result from our expectation and actuals. There's a variance between the expected amount and the actual gross accounts receivable for the current yea. I do a quick scan and search my support and think if I have been made aware of anything that would help me explain the reason for this difference. One possibility could be that the recent downturn of the market has decreased sales and thus lead to a decrease in accounts receivables. Another possibility is that the client's competitors may have established more favorable credit terms, thus reducing business for the client. I chalk these down as possibilities, so I can suggest reasons for the variance, which would make me, sound intelligent in front of the client. I write a reminder note to myself that I will have to follow up with the client.

4:30pm - My 4:30pm appointment is here, but the client is still on the phone when I walk by her cubical. How rude I think to myself, but as auditors we are mostly numb to this by now, so I quickly dismiss it. I wait for the client to get off the phone.

4:35pm - She finally has time to and gets right to the point and asks what I need from her. I told her that I need the support that I've been asking for the past week or so. I scan my list of follow up questions and note that I have a few for her. I fire away and quickly make notes of the client's responses. Further, I try to gain an understanding of when to expect the support. The reason I push is because I know my senior will push me and ask me why I have not received the support. As a way to cover my bases, I push the client a little bit.

5:00pm - I get back to the audit conference room and notice that it is already 5:00pm. Unfortunately it is busy season and we are only half way done with the day. I hope to get out by 10:00pm. I've been assigned to take care of dinner. Luckily for me we use an outside delivery service. All I have to do is pick the restaurant and then the service will send each of my team members an email in which they will be able to order from a menu. After they place their orders, it will send the orders to the selected restaurant and a driver will deliver the food to us at a specified time. I arrange for the email to be sent to my team members.

6:00pm - I continue to audit and document my understanding that I gained from the client. I scan the database and see that the senior has left me coaching notes. One of the coaching notes pertains to if we have performed a bucketing test for the AR aging or not. I document that in the scoping document in step 9210, we deemed it unnecessary as we have controls reliance over the system report. I ask the senior if he has time to go over some of the other coaching notes he has left for me.

8:00pm - By now all the client contacts have left for the day. It's just the audit team and the janitors now. Our food arrives on time and the engagement team takes over a difference conference room to have dinner. We take about thirty minutes to eat dinner. It is a good break from the computer screen. One of the associates asks if anyone has any big plans for the weekend. He obviously is unaware of the fact that the entire time will be working through the weekend. That is quite alright because the senior quickly reminds him of this.

8:30pm - It's time to get back to the computer. Now that the client has left, I have time to do some more audit work. I also update my list of follow up questions and note the progress to the right of each line item. I document all that I can with what I've learned from the client and continue to do detail testing for my cash steps. Yet another status update with the senior and at this point, I've amassed a list of questions for my senior as well. Many of which include the testing approaches we are taking this year. Others are simply documentation preference questions- whether or not he wants the step description as well as the step number in the documentation.

10:30pm - I still have a lot on my plate and a billion neurons firing at once in my brain. Suddenly, I am reminded of having to follow up on support I received from a contact located in New York. As there is a three hour time difference between the east coast and west coast, I will have to call the contact at 7:00am tomorrow to reach them at 10:00am. It looks like an early morning tomorrow.

11:30pm - The entire team is still in the conference room. So much for leaving at 10:00pm today, I think to myself. I make sure that I have all my questions listed for the client tomorrow and have sent out the necessary e-mails. I have audited to the extent, which I can with the given time. My senior tells me to go home. Out of courtesy, I ask the entire team if there is anything I can help with. Nobody is going to give me additional work at this hour, so I take off.

1:00am - I get back home and get ready for bed. Within seconds, I knock out.

Is Big 4 experience overrated?

What benefits do you receive from working these incredibly insane hours?

I can tell you that you will not be compensated financially to the level you expect. But, without a doubt after it is all said and done, you will have grown significantly both in terms of people skills and technical accounting knowledge. Each client poses a different challenge and at times you will feel almost as if even though you took two steps forward, you probably also took three steps back. The moment you feel like you've grounded yourself on auditing methodology and think you understand what needs to be accomplished, new issues will arise and your cumulative knowledge might leave you ill prepared to resolve the issue. In other words, you are constantly learning and being pushed into waters which you have not yet navigated before. It's a grind and unfortunately or fortunately enough, you'll have to string together days and push through.

So why is working at a Big 4 so challenging? Well, to summarize, it is a grown man/woman career.

You are required to communicate with controllers, managers, and high level executives to gain an understanding of their business. Furthermore, you have a specified time frame to develop that understanding to the extent in which you can document it and communicate to individuals who are not working on your areas in a clear and concise manner. On top of all of that, having come right out of college, you are expected to understand the accounting technicalities. At the same time, the individuals/companies you audit have experience upwards toward twenty plus years. In that respect, there is a huge learning curve. Individuals on a team have assigned 'steps' or standard procedures you perform, however it's not as simple as ABC. If you have no experience with auditing you will not be able to follow these procedures.

The reason is that these procedures are written out for individuals who have audit experience! As a first year you gain exposure to cash, property, plant, and equipment, accounts payable, and various less risky areas. You start to gain a grasp of accounting in practice and you begin to realize that it's not as straightforward as it was written in your college textbooks.

You'll start to see that the excel files your client work with are unorganized and difficult to decipher. For someone who is not already familiar with the excel file, they can be extremely difficult to follow. They have numbers all over the place and numbers that are hardcoded. There is no manual or guide as to what is going on with the spreadsheet. The only way to gain an understanding over it is to have the client explain to you or have a senior associate coach you.

Effectively you are checking the work of some let us say forty year old manager who has tons more experience than you do and actually has a clue of what is going on. How do you think they feel when you come in and challenge their work?

I can't imagine anyone who welcomes auditors. You'll get push back from the client more times than not, but they understand the audit doesn't get done if they don't cooperate with you. Still, for whatever reason, they will make it as difficult for you as possible. My biggest advice I can give is to research the topic to get background on the issue before you speak to the client. This can be looking at prior year databases, firm research resources, and asking your senior.

What is the average age in Big 4 accounting?

One of the most commonly asked questions I get is: "Am I too old/young for Big 4 Public Accounting?" The short answer to this is no, but of course if you are outside of the typical range it may be more difficult for you to break in.

The average employee age in "Big 4 accounting firms" ranges from around 25 to 35 years. While the majority of the firm is made up of associates, partners' ages range from the early 30s to late 50s. This in it itself raises the average age.

Here is an approximate break out by age is estimated as follows:

New Associates/Staff	20yrs-25yrs
Experienced Associates/Staff	21yrs-27yrs
Senior Associates	24yrs-32yrs
Managers	29yrs-36yrs
Senior Managers	30yrs+
Partners	30yrs+

The fact of the matter is Big 4 firms hire directly from undergraduate college/university campuses. This means that they are hiring individuals in their early 20s. However, in some cases, people start college later or begin working after they've obtained a Masters in Accounting. In order to become a CPA, some states require you to have a specified amount of semester units, which can naturally translate into a Master's degree. This along with any breaks you take outside of the typical four years college experience will evidently add to your age. The fact of the matter is regardless of your age, if you are a senior in college, they are looking to hire you for a full-time position.

The alternative route to breaking into the Big 4 is to come in as an experienced hire. Often times, the Big 4 end up hiring from other Big 4 firms. The way they get you to come from a KPMG to PwC is by throwing more money at you.

But more commonly, the Big 4 poach from lesser tier auditing firms such as BDO Seidman or a Grant Thornton. Evidently this skews the average age of the firm.

Most often than not, those hired into the firm from mid-tier or local firms are demoted a position. For example, suppose you were hired from a mid-tier firm. At that firm you were a manager, but at a Big 4 they may offer you the senior associate role with the opportunity to be promoted in the following year. Despite the fact that auditing in general is all the same, firm methodologies do differ slightly. This extra year gives you a chance to catch up to those who have worked within the firm for multiple years and therefore are more familiar with firm methodologies.

You'll notice that there is not a big age gap between the different levels within the firm. Yes the difference between an associate versus a partner can be 20+yrs, but generally speaking the age of a senior associate and a manager is only about three to six years apart. This is due to the promotional structure in Big 4. They are limited liability partnerships and assume an apprenticeship model. Therefore, you are up for promotion after two to three years. Whether or not you get promoted is dependent on need and your qualifications.

There is almost a natural progression from new associate to experienced associate after your first year. As you move up the ladder, it becomes more and more difficult to advance. However, if your reviews are in line with/exceed expectations, these advances should come naturally. If your goal is to make partner at the firm, you should know that it will not be an easy task. While progression can generally be more or less expected from associate to senior associate, being on the partner track requires more than just meeting expectations. In the past, it used to be that if you paid your dues with the number of years (at least 10 years) you've been with the firm, you would become a partner. However, nowadays most firms require that you have specialized in an industry or have had unique experiences. For example, having done an overseas tour or a tour in the national office would be examples of unique experiences.

The attrition rate is high in public accounting and especially in the Big 4. For instance, if twenty people were hired as new associates, about fifteen would remain after the second year. After about the senior year, I would say about five would remain. Typically at the senior level, people usually know whether or not public accounting is for them. Also it is a convenient cut off point for people who are looking for better work life balance. When you start to get towards the manager, senior manager, and partner level, you are looking at maybe two or three individuals left in your start class. The firm actually depends on this model because; of course we can't have three managers to three associates. This helps the business model in which typically people are promoted after two years.

Which office or location should you choose?

Contrary to popular belief, it does matter which office and location you chose to work at. Now most people would elect to work at the most convenient office. That may be the office closest to where they live or an office close to where they went school to. Whatever it may be, it is still important to understand that although we are all one firm and the overall cultural is relatively consistent, there are differences between locations. For example, not all offices are the same size. New York is a lot bigger than the Phoenix office. You can image the people are different as well. While New York would most likely service financial services clients such as Goldman Sachs, the Phoenix office may service companies like Honeywell. Though they are both big companies, they are in different industries and are of different sizes. In LA, you would most likely be servicing the entertainment industry.

In a big office, there might be a thousand plus individuals. You may be a small fish in a big pond. More likely than not, there will be a lot of new faces even after being in the firm for a couple years.

Contrast that with a smaller office of let us say 300 people. In a smaller office, you might know everyone at least by face. It comes down to if you want that small office feel with that big office name or the big office feel. Alternatively you can think of it as being one fish in a big pond or one fish in a small pond.

Some factors you should consider while determining the location you decide to work at include:

1) Convenience of commute time to work
2) If you enjoy being at the location
3) Significant others' work location
4) Clients and industry you wish to work on
5) Size of the office you wish to work in

As an auditor you typically do not work in the firm's office unless you are doing planning or something that does not intensively involve the client. Most firms will not have much office space and if they do most of it is for their consulting or tax services employees. We are typically at the client's site 70% of the time we would work from there. Depending on what job you are on, the client may or may not designate a cubical for you. Typically you and your team will work in a conference room. There might be five of you sharing one conference room table. You can image all the wires and laptops on the table. It can get a bit messy. On the other hand, a coworker of mine is always at this one client year round. She gets her own cubical and hours are more manageable as you can predict which times will be busy and which times you will not be busy. This is in comparison to if you were on multiple jobs at multiple periods of time. In this case, you would be working with multiple managers across multiple jobs. Most likely, your managers will not coordinate between each other. Therefore you become the hub and the person who needs to keep your managers informed of your workload on other jobs.

How much traveling will you be able to do?

Where you end up traveling to is largely dependent on your engagements (job assignment) and where the firm needs you to be. For our purposes, let us consider traveling as going to a city other than that of which your home office resides.

If you wish to travel, the earlier in your career you make it known to others, the better the firm can accommodate your request. Some people travel more than others and then you have people who don't travel at all. As a first year, generally speaking you can expect to be traveling about 0-30% of the year.

Personally, my travels have typically been within California. However, there are opportunities for international travel. A couple of years back, I did spend some time in Canada. A colleague of mine travelled to New York, Boston, Arizona, Oregon, and even the UK for work.

Typically larger clients will have more travel opportunities than smaller client because the larger clients are more likely to have multiple offices. However, a client with multiple offices does not always guarantee travel to those locations. For cost efficiency purposes, if the company you are auditing has multiple offices, typically the firm will have the local office perform audit procedures versus sending someone from the corporate audit team. The corporate audit team is the engagement team auditing the client's corporate offices. Sometimes, the client may request that the corporate team also be involved in the audits of the other locations. In this case, the firm may send you to various client offices.

One of the reasons why the client prefers this is for consistency purposes. The client would rather have someone who has knowledge of their corporate accounting practices audit their other locations than someone without that knowledge.

This limits the number of questions we will ask as we are already familiar with the client's business. The best way to find out which jobs have travel and which ones do not is to ask the seniors on the jobs or people in your office.

Travel opportunities differ as you move up the firm. As a first year, firms send you wherever there is a need. It is not unusual to be on more than ten jobs your first year at various lengths of time. Typically an engagement can last anywhere from a week to several months. For larger jobs, you are typically on the client year round. As you move through the firm and into your second and third years, you begin to focus on fewer clients. By the time you are a senior at the firm, depending on your industry, you may have one or two larger clients or five smaller clients.

Every year, the firm offers trainings for your level. Typically they will send you somewhere different from your local office for regional training. In the past, firms have sent people to places such as Arizona, Texas, and Illinois for about a week or two. They will put you in a hotel and you will be able to expense your meals and car rental. There will be more on firms sponsored trainings in a little bit.

One of the reasons why the client prefers this is for consistency purposes. The client would rather have someone who has knowledge of their corporate accounting practices audit their other locations than someone without that knowledge.

Opportunities to work for long periods of time (more than a month) outside of your home country typically are not presented to you until you are promoted to senior. Employees are eligible for two to three year tours once they become a senior. Meaning you would work overseas for two or three years and then come back to your home office. The purpose of these firm tours is so that you can share your experiences. It also helps build your network and helps you grow professionally and personally. Not everyone will be eligible to participate in an overseas tour. But those who are high performers typically have the choice to do so. Popular tour locations include Europe, Asia, or Australia. While you are able to express your interest as to where you would like to do your tour, sometimes it is dependent on need. The firm will set up the paperwork and you will be paid in local currency. These are great experiences to learn about different cultures and provide growth opportunities.

As a manager, senior manager, or partner, there are more opportunities to travel internationally. As you may have guessed this is due to the fact that you will be primarily managing and building relationships to garner business. Just so you have some perspective, a manager once told me that she has been in over thirty countries as a result of the opportunities at the firm. Traveling frequency is dependent again on client needs – after all we are in the client services business.

While it may sound glorious at first, traveling does take its toll. This is especially the case when you are out of town for multiple weeks and away from your family. The first couple days are great especially if you arrive on a weekend and have time to explore the city. But by the end of the trip, most people will learn that traveling for work is different from traveling for leisure.

When you begin to travel you'llunderstand that it is to your advantage to pack light. There are a couple tricks that I've learned along the way. For example, for week long trips, typically one carry on suitcase is enough for all my business and casual clothes. This means that when the airplane lands, you don't have to wait on the carrousel for your luggage. As a result, you saved at least thirty minutes to an hour off your trip both ways. Not to mention the risk of loss of luggage is reduced as you know that you've stored your luggage in the overhead compartment.

On one of my traveling trips, I arrived Sunday night at 8:00pm with my team in Scottsdale, Arizona. Depending on your situation you may arrive as a team or individually. For the duration of our trip, we rented a car to carpool to work. For convenience, we would also book the same hotel. Travel meals are business expenses, so it is not uncommon from team to eat together for dinner in the city. Essentially as a result of traveling, you spend most of the day with the team. While it is not mandatory that you eat with your team; people usually do to show that they are a team player. On the weekends, the firm will fly you back. Alternatively, I know that there are some firms that will let you fly someone in and out if you elected not to fly back. The reason this is allowed is because it is the same price to the firm either way. In certain situations, the manager may allow you to expense the hotel; otherwise it is your cost during the weekend.

Every year the firm will provide live formal training for you to help you step into your industry. Therefore, you may be asked to step up in an acting senior role after only working a year and a half in firm. This evidently depends on the circumstances; typically they will find a senior to fill a senior role, but not always. These formal trainings help prepare you for the coming year and your new role with the firm. As you may be aware already, there is high turnover in the public accounting.

These training are usually a week long. In the past, firms would organize these regionally. For example, if you were based in Minneapolis, Minnesota or Columbus, Ohio, you might attend a regional training held in Chicago. Not only did this give you an opportunity to travel without the normal pressures that come with having to meet client demands, but also to meet people from different areas. However, firms have since moved to more local trainings to cut costs. In private accounting, the trainings are not as formalized. More times than not, it is up to you to seek training opportunities. It is more common to only have on the job training in private accounting than anything formalized.

Unlike traveling for a client, most firms will have you share hotel rooms when traveling for training especially if you are a new associate. Trainings are held in usually held in conference rooms in large groups. Depending on your level, you will likely have someone above you teaching the course. For example, for first and second years you'd typically have seniors or managers within the firm teaching the courses. From my experience, training topics typically cover a mix of soft skills and technical skills. Evidently there is more focus on audit techniques and the firm's audit methodology.

Soft skills comes more into play as you move up the ladder and become a senior. The curriculum usually involves some level of group interaction. Usually we given a question/scenario/task and then we will split into table groups and work together to come up with a solution or audit approach to present to the overall group. What I enjoy about these trainings is that it is more interactive than say only listening to a lecturer.

Training schedules are usually generous with fitting in regular breaks. This means we end up on average staying in training for less than eight hours a day. If it is a Friday, it is even shorter as it is likely that people will have to try to catch flights back home before 5:00PM. This gives people who are from out of town an opportunity to get back home at a decent time.

In addition to offsite trainings, the firms offer numerous online trainings. These are mostly offered through the firms' intranet and most of them are web-based. This is where you will get most of your technical trainings outside of learning on the job. The intranets offer a wide variety of courses to take ranging from audit to tax to consulting. They dive deeper into different financial statement line items and their inherent risks. For example, it would not be difficult to find trainings on how to account for inventory or understanding the nuances with stock-based compensation. It is a great way to build your knowledge going into busy season. They can range anywhere from thirty minutes to eight hours per training course.

Occasionally, managers will hold training session on specific topics. These are also helpful in learning more about the technical accounting pronouncements including the various ASC codifications. These help associates and seniors familiarize with the areas they will be auditing. Normally they are only a couple hours long and if they are nice they will provide lunch.

Based on my experience from interning at Boeing and working at several other mid- market companies, on the job training at a Big 4 is probably one of the best ways to learn. Not only are you given a great deal of responsibility as a first year, but you are also given the opportunity to grow within the firm both professionally and personally. The tight deadlines and strong demands of this job shape you to become more organized and efficient in your work.

For example, for public companies they have specific hard deadlines for when they are looking to release their quarterly review report or as we call it the 10Q. All the review work would need to be finished before then, but at the same time we cannot begin field work until the client has closed their books. Evidently, this presents time constraints and the need to be efficient to meet the deadlines.

What is going on with outsourcing services? Will you be out of a job?

You've heard of outsourcing manufacturing of specific products, but what about outsourcing professional services? Outsourcing services is become more and more common as companies look to reduce costs.

How does the process work? Audit teams will coordinate requests through a web/software based infrastructure to Argentina or India based teams. Engagement teams will provide instructions on how to perform the audit procedures, examples of previous work products, timelines, and schedule of deliverables. Instructions needs to be detailed, otherwise the oversea teams will not understand what the final work product is expected to look like.

There have been some frustrations in the early stages of utilizing this outsourcing model. For example, individuals have complained about how it is largely inefficient to instruct someone a thousand miles away on how to follow up on a confirmation not received. Often times, it would take engagement teams more time to prepare the instructions than for them to perform the work themselves.

Specifically Big 4 accounting firms are moving some of the work that a first year would typically do to overseas delivery centers. As a first year, some of your duties include sending out bank confirmations and tying out the 10-K. Though there has been a debate as to whether or not outsourcing these services is efficient, firms are determined to make it work and have continued to leverage this business model.

How does the process work? Audit teams will coordinate requests through a web/software based infrastructure to Argentina or India based teams. Engagement teams will provide instructions on how to perform the audit procedures, examples of previous work products, timelines, and schedule of deliverables. Instructions needs to be detailed, otherwise the oversea teams will not understand what the final work product is expected to look like.

There have been some frustrations in the early stages of utilizing this outsourcing model. For example, individuals have complained about how it is largely inefficient to instruct someone a thousand miles away on how to follow up on a confirmation not received. Often times, it would take engagement teams more time to prepare the instructions than for them to perform the work themselves.

Employees have made the argument that outsourcing these activities takes away from the first year's learning experience. However, the flip side argument is that the learning will occur when he or she is managing the process. In addition, in the long run the outsourced team will learn how to perform the task faster and with fewer instructions. The goal is to have the local Big 4 team members coach, monitor, and review these tasks. As a result, through this process the local Big 4 team member will be able to save time and also focus on more complex tasks all the while still understanding the tasks being performed by the external location.

My recommendation is to embrace the outsourcing. As a new staff, if you volunteer to manage the process, that will only make you that much valuable to the team. The truth of the matter is the senior will pawn off that work to you anyways, so volunteering to manage the process will only score you brownie points.

What are cycle counts and physical inventory observations?

One of the ways we get comfortable over the inventory balance or rather the existence of it is to go on site and actually see it/count it. The firms have methodology for how to determine which warehouses and how many counts to observe. Companies will typically have one or two methods to count their inventory. One is performing regular inventory cycle counts. Every day, week, month, or however often they will count X amount of inventory.

The alternative is a full physical inventory count which is done once a year at the end of the year. In both cases, warehouse or inventory employees will have a blind count sheet (showing only the items to be counted for that day). He or she will then go around and count/weigh/measure the inventory. Depending on the company they may have TVs, IPods, or Laptops. These are the easy things to count because you can see one TV and one IPod. I've had to count/weight pillow stuffing/cases, cars, nuts and bolts, resin, and computer parts. My coworkers have had to weigh sand. There was a client in Hawaii and apparently the sand there is very valuable to company. There was literally a pile of sand worth about a million dollars sitting outside the company's door.

One difference between a cycle count and a physical inventory count is the number of instances you would observe. With cycle counts you would be observing more than one, while a physical inventory count you would be doing it once a year.

If you do not know already some of these cycle counts can be brutal. When I say brutal I mean waking up at 2am to get on site at 4am to do the cycle count. During Thanksgiving break and specifically the days leading up to Black Friday, I was assigned multiple cycle counts. Now typically the counts are done before shipping or receiving comes in and out of the warehouse, otherwise you would have varying counts between what is in the system and what is on hand. For example, let's say you count three TVs, but two seconds later you ship out two TVs, well then what you just counted would be incorrect. For some reason, the engagement team decided to do these counts during the busiest time of the year for computers and TVs. I literally had to sleep at 10:00 PM on a Wednesday to wake up at 2:00 AM to drive two hours to the middle of nowhere. For your information, warehouse are usually in the middle of nowhere because that's where there is a lot of open space. Then from there I would spend about three hours counting things with the employees and performing other procedures. By the time I was done it would be about seven in the morning or so. I think to myself, this is great timing.

This is exactly the time when there would be traffic because everyone is going to work. So, when I leave it takes me about two hours to get to the city I work in. Then, I have another full day at the client site.

When you think of physical inventory observations think of end of the year. This means you may be booked to count things during Christmas week or even the day before New Year's.

If you are lucky you might be able to do this with several other people. Otherwise it is typically just you. They put a lot of responsibility on the new hires and second years, who are the ones that typically get scheduled on these. This includes scheduling with the client and understanding what procedures need to be performed. Then executing them and providing deliverables to the senior. The senior or experienced associate will provide you with instructions on what to get from the client and procedures. Also, if you are onsite and have questions they will be reachable via the telephone. Don't get me wrong, sometimes it's nice if you are counting inventory during the weekday because these typically do not take eight hours. But more likely than not, these inventory counts are done on the weekends where there is no shipping or receiving happening. I've actually had to count women's clothing on super bowl day. It was one of the worst inventory experiences. That Sunday, we spent about 5 hours counting every piece of clothing and accessory in a retail store. At the end of it all, we found errors and had to recount. I ended up leaving at 1AM. My advice is to make sure you count it correctly the first time!

What do teams usually do for lunch?

Some people bring their lunch either a sandwich or food in Tupperware; others will buy lunch, or just eat a quick snack. Regardless of who you work most teams will usually eats together. This may differ depending on your work location. While it is not required, it is almost always done unless of course you have another obligation. For example, if you were meeting a friend for lunch or had a doctor's appointment during lunch then you would be "let off the hook". A typical lunch would be in front of the computer in the conference room with your colleagues. However, to mix it up sometimes we will eat outside, which is obviously my preference. Usually the senior makes the call based on how much work he or she believes has to get done.

If you think our lunches are anywhere near an hour, you are sadly mistaken. These are quick twenty to at most thirty minute lunches. There are evidently exceptions to this rule, on bigger jobs where you are on the job year round and have your own cubical, the senior may be a bit more lax and let his or her associates take lunch whenever. When the partner or manager visits, they might take the team out for lunch. These lunches are a lot longer; about an hour. On those days the team usually doesn't get much done because the partner will dab into the database, begin to look over the team's work, and ask questions. Generally speaking, there isn't that much time for lunch and even when we finish lunch we know that there is a lot of work to be done.

How many vacation days or paid time off do you get?

While it will vary slightly between the Big 4 firms, generally speaking they are generous with vacation days. On average I would say in the first two years at the firm you'll have about fifteen days of vacation a year. That comes out to a vacation accrual rate of ten hours per month. Also you can think about it as having three weeks of vacation. After your second year with the firm, you'll have about twenty two days of vacation, which works out to be just over four weeks of vacation or paid time off! This is not including holidays whether they are firm or national. How does this compare to working at in the accounting department of a large firm such as General Electric? Generally speaking, if you were to work in industry, firms will give you two weeks of vacation.

Hold your horses!

Like with many good deals there is almost always a catch. We don't always get all the holidays off. For example, Veteran's Day and Martin Luther King Day we don't get off. However, the firms will slightly make up for this through additional firm holidays. For example, the day before Thanksgiving we have off. Certain years, due to seasonality of our business, the firms will give three days off the week of Christmas and in exchange ask that you take two days of vacation. So essentially if you count holidays and vacation days, you can effectively have more than a month off.

Sometimes firms will allow you to go into the vacation negative. This means you can effectively take more vacation than you have accrued.

However, while it is not written in stone, there is a widely known rule that you are not allowed to take vacation during busy season. Busy season is technically the time from January through the end of March. Also, it is not smiled upon to book vacation during quarterly reviews. This is the time right after quarter-end close. For instance, for a 12/31 year-ended client, the second week of April would be when the quarter one review would begin.

Aside from vacation days, firms usually have a sabbatical program in place. Because it is typically not as busy as it is during the summer as it is the first four months of the year, firms will allow you to go on temporary leave for a couple of months with little to no pay. Depending on the situation, I've had co-workers who have taken advantage of this program and gone on trips overseas. It is great to be able to leave for a couple months, but to still have a job when you come back. I'm fairly certain that most other companies would not permit this.

We want to know how much money you make and what drives your salary. Different firms have different way of rating their employees. Generally speaking if you are on a job for more than eighty hours you will request for a performance review from your senior or in the case of a senior the manager and so on and so forth. These feedback reviews are designed to help create a portfolio for your case for a bonus, raise, or promotion at the end of the year.

There are a couple parts to the review. As an associate you will submit to your senior what you helped with, completed, and basically did on the engagement. Then describe what you have learned during your couple weeks or months on the engagement. Finally, you'll identify some weaknesses or areas where you can improve. The senior will write a review of your performance and give you a rating. Depending on the firm you might have ratings like below expectations, met expectations, or exceeded expectations. Different people have different expectations and as a first year it is pretty difficult to get exceeded expectations. The reason is that you are pretty much learning as you are going along. The only way you would be able to get exceeded is if you perform duties that are above your level.

Usually after the senior writes your review they will send it back to you to review or discuss. Then you sign off or talk about areas you'd like to change to reflect what you truly did or what not. It's generally difficult to remember what you do on a job after you roll off the job and move on to another job. What, I would recommend is to take notes during your engagement and identify specific things that you've worked on.

There are other things that factor into your review process. For example if you worked on a special project for a manager, you can add that to your portfolio. I had some open time in my schedule so one of my managers asked that I help compile some data for a finance guy on the other side of the coast. I worked with him extensively for a couple weeks. After that time I asked him to write me a note of my performance, which I included in my review portfolio.

Another thing that can be added to your portfolio is if you had worked on setting up events within the firm to promote connectivity or if there was something that was not captured in your performance reviews. For example, you could have prepared the monthly newsletter or something that is outside of normal audit work.

At the end of the day your ratings (e.g. 1 – high performer, 2-performing, 3- performing below) give you a bonus or slight salary bump. I would say the difference between a 1 and a 3 is no more than $5,000 on the associate level. It becomes complex as you move up and is more variable.

How much money will you make?

Isn't this just a popular question? I will tell you straight out and upfront that you will not become a millionaire working at a Big 4 in your first couple years. Is it possible during your lifetime? I think so granted inflation reduces the true value of your money. But the fact is that you won't see the big bucks until you hit senior manager and probably partner. That is a long path and usually not guaranteed.

Alright now let's get to some of the numbers. Your salary is dependent on your location as your cost of living may vary, whether or not you have a master's degree, and if there was some kind of sign-on bonus. Typically previous interns will receive sign-on bonuses. This is because firms have already invested a great deal in you and would like to keep talent.

These are relatively rough estimates and are likely to change year over year, but generally speaking these are the ranges.

New associates - $50-$63k
Seniors – $64K – 79k
Managers -80s-100s
Partners – 250k+

What percent raise does one receive year over year? Historically these raises have been large percentages. They range from the high single digits to low double digits (~9% to~ 20%). Still, I would argue our base is very low to begin with. In other industries, there are a lot of people who start off making $60k or $70k in other industries. Bonuses in your first few years at the firm usually do not exceed $5,000.

www.ingramcontent.com/pod-product-compliance
Lightning Source LLC
Chambersburg PA
CBHW041207180526
45172CB00006B/1215

* 9 7 8 1 4 8 1 0 9 7 0 4 8 *